D1568669

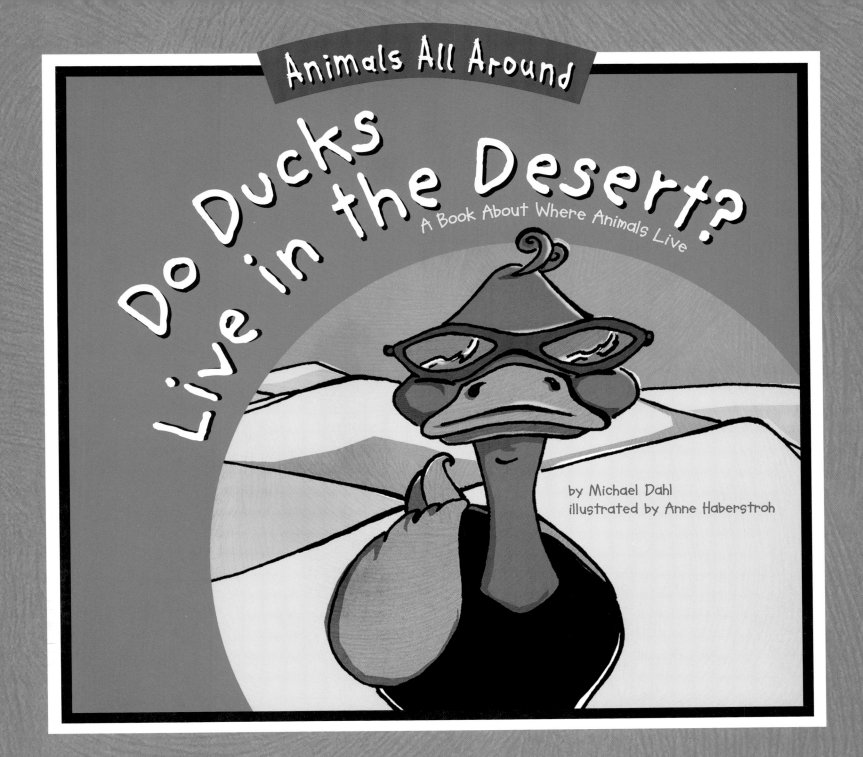

Animals All Around

Do Ducks Live in the Desert?
A Book About Where Animals Live

by Michael Dahl
illustrated by Anne Haberstroh

Special thanks to our advisers for their expertise:

Kathleen E. Hunt, Ph.D.
Research Scientist & Lecturer, Zoology Department
University of Washington, Seattle, Washington

Susan Kesselring, M.A., Literacy Educator
Rosemount-Apple Valley-Eagan (Minnesota) School District

PICTURE WINDOW BOOKS
MINNEAPOLIS, MINNESOTA

Managing Editor: Bob Temple
Creative Director: Terri Foley
Editor: Peggy Henrikson
Editorial Adviser: Andrea Cascardi
Copy Editor: Laurie Kahn
Designer: Todd Ouren
Page production: Picture Window Books
The illustrations in this book were rendered digitally.

Picture Window Books
5115 Excelsior Boulevard
Suite 232
Minneapolis, MN 55416
1-877-845-8392
www.picturewindowbooks.com

Printed in the United States of America.

Library of Congress Cataloging-in-Publication Data
Dahl, Michael.
Do ducks live in the desert? : a book about where animals live / by Michael Dahl ;
illustrated by Anne Haberstroh.
p. cm. — (Animals all around)
Summary: Presents a variety of animals and the different places in which they live.
Includes bibliographical references and index.
ISBN 1-4048-0290-8 (Lib. Bdg.)
1. Animals — Juvenile literature. 2. Habitat (Ecology) — Juvenile literature.
[1. Habitat (Ecology) 2. Animals. 3. Ecology.]
I. Haberstroh, Anne, ill. II. Title.
QL49 .D313 2004
590 — dc22
                                        2003018262

Do ducks live in the desert?

No! Ducks live in wetlands.

Ducks called redheads build their nests among tall wetland grasses. Redheads waddle through the mucky mud of marshes and paddle in the shallow water. They dunk their heads to nibble on water plants. They snap up bugs with their busy bills.

Do musk oxen live in the desert?

No! Musk oxen live on the tundra.

Herds of musk oxen graze on flat or rolling tundra in the cold, windy north. In the winter, temperatures drop below freezing. Ice covers the ground. Hungry musk oxen use their sharp horns and hooves to dig through the ice. Then they can munch on the dried plants beneath.

6

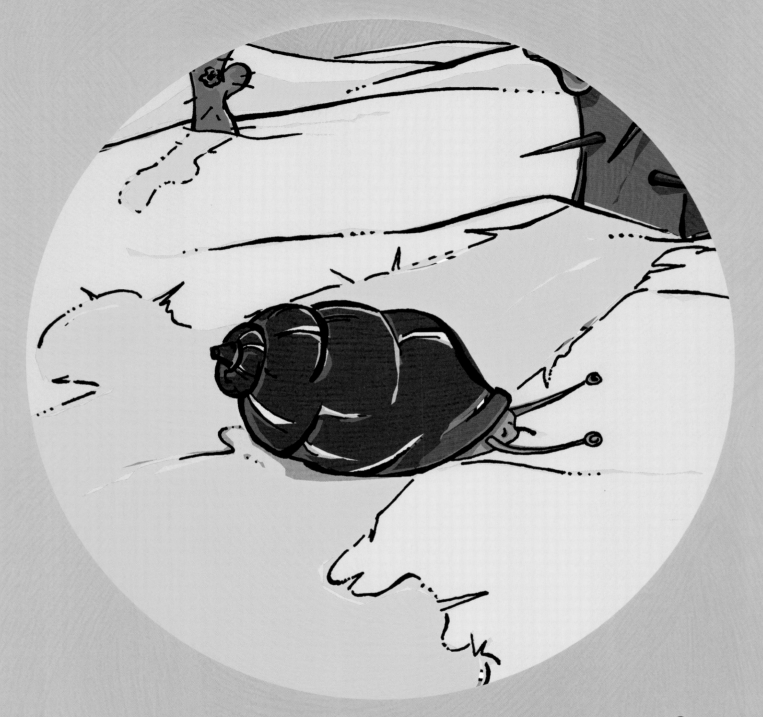

Do periwinkles live in the desert?

No! Periwinkles live on seashore rocks.

Periwinkle snails hatch from tiny eggs in the salty sea. Snails are carried up the shore with each high tide. When the tide goes out, the periwinkles cling to rocks along the shore. They eat the slick slime that grows on the wet rocks.

Do meadowlarks live in the desert?

No! Meadowlarks live on the Prairie.

Male meadowlarks perch on tall grasses in the prairie.
They sit on fence posts and lift their yellow throats to sing.
Their flute-like songs tell other males to stay away.
Female meadowlarks build nests hidden in the prairie grass.

Do sloths live in the desert?

No! Sloths live in the tropical rain forest.

Slow, sleepy sloths hang from the branches of rain-forest trees. Tiny green plants grow on the sloths' long, damp fur. This makes the animals blend in with the leaves. Sloths can't move fast to escape enemies, but their color helps them hide.

Do water striders live in the desert?

No! Water striders live on a pond.

A water strider skims across the top of a pond. Its waterproof feet only make tiny dents in the surface of the water. The strider uses its middle legs to push itself along. Its back legs are for steering and stopping. The short front legs are for catching smaller bugs to eat.

Do octopuses live in the desert?

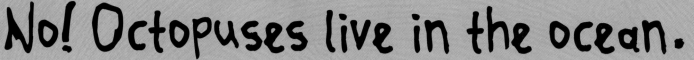

No! Octopuses live in the ocean.

The blue ring octopus hides among coral reefs in tropical oceans. Its bright blue rings show up only when the animal is frightened. Divers enjoying the colorful reefs must be careful. This octopus bites if it's disturbed, and its powerful poison can be deadly.

16

Do moles live in the desert?

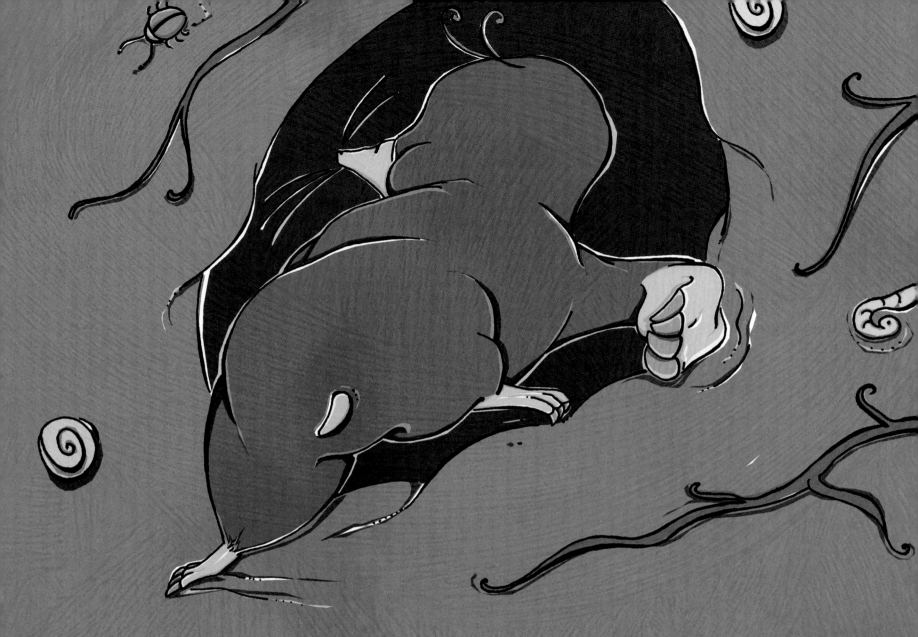

No! Moles live in dirt tunnels.

Moles dig tunnels in the dark dirt with their wide front feet and big claws. A mole's eyes are tiny. The animal uses its nose and whiskers to feel for worms and insects to eat. A mole can easily move forward or backward in its tunnel.

Do markhors live in the desert?

No! Markhors live in the mountains.

Markhors are wild goats that live in the high mountains of south central Asia. In summer, the goats graze on grass. In winter, they climb down the mountain until they find trees with twigs and leaves. Markhors are endangered because hunters prize the animals' curling horns.

Do camels live in the desert?

Yes! Camels live in the desert.

Camels do well in the desert. Camel nostrils close in the sandy desert wind. Long, thick eyelashes keep sand out of the camels' eyes. Wide, padded feet keep the animals from sinking into the soft sand. Camels store fat in their humps, so they can walk for a long time without eating.

Where Animals Live

Some animals live mostly on the water.

redhead ducks   wetlands

water striders   ponds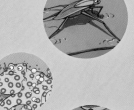

Some animals live in the water.

blue ring octopuses   ocean

periwinkle snails   seashore rocks

Some animals live underground.

moles   dirt tunnels

Some animals live in flat or gently rolling places.

musk oxen   tundra

meadowlarks   prairies

Some animals live in high places.

sloths   rain-forest trees

markhors   mountain slopes

Some animals live in hot, dry places.

camels   deserts

Glossary

coral reef — a long ridge or pile of many shapes and colors created by the hard skeletons of tiny sea creatures. Coral can look like underwater flowers or plants.

endangered — in danger. An endangered species is a type of animal or plant that is in danger of being totally wiped out. Sometimes laws are made to protect endangered species.

prairie — a flat or rolling area of tall grasses and few or no trees

rain forest — a very thick, green forest that grows in rainy, tropical areas

tide — the rising and falling of the ocean up and down the shore. There are usually two high tides and two low tides in 24 hours, or one day.

tropical — having to do with the very hot area around the outer middle of the earth

tundra — an area of flat or rolling plains in the far north. The tundra has no trees but has mosses and other low plants growing in its cold, damp soil.

wetland — an area that has very wet soil, tall marsh grasses, and often shallow water

Index

To Learn More

At the Library

Ashman, Linda. *Castles, Caves, and Honeycombs*. San Diego: Harcourt, 2001.

Hewitt, Sally. *All Kinds of Habitats*. New York: Children's Press, 1999.

Richardson, Adele D. *Wetlands*. Mankato, Minn.: Bridgestone Books, 2001.

Taylor, Barbara. *Animal Hide and Seek*. New York: DK Pub., 1998.

Wilkins, Sally. *Deserts*. Mankato, Minn.: Bridgestone Books, 2001.

On the Web

Fact Hound offers a safe, fun way to find Web sites related to this book. All of the sites on Fact Hound have been researched by our staff.
http://www.facthound.com

1. Visit the Fact Hound home page.
2. Enter a search word related to this book, or type in this special code: 1404802908.
3. Click on the FETCH IT button.

Your trusty Fact Hound will fetch the best sites for you!